T0157108

RHYMES

in the

LIVES *of* WOMEN

Laarni Manalac-Fajardo

author HOUSE®

AuthorHouse™
1663 Liberty Drive
Bloomington, IN 47403
www.authorhouse.com
Phone: 1-800-839-8640

Published by AuthorHouse   10/10/2012

ISBN: 978-1-4772-3461-7 (sc)
ISBN: 978-1-4772-3462-4 (e)

*"The BEAUTY of a woman
is NOT in the clothes she wears,
the figures that she carries,
or the way she combs her hair . . .
The BEAUTY of a woman
must be seen in her eyes . . .
because that is the doorway
to her HEART . . .
The place where
LOVE resides!"
(Unknown)*

FOREWORD

It must have all started in secondary school
Learning about Literature . . .
That my interest in verses and poems is kindled
Innocently knowing . . . my inkling is growing . . . .

I've always been captivated by verses & poems
loving what they mean . . . enticed with each word
after so many moons . . . it just dawned on me . . . .
thoughts & feelings . . . pouring out from me . . . .

Alas! I'm writing my very own . . . .
It's freedom, passion, love . . . and ALL!

And now, it brings me joy . . .
To warm your heart, uplift your spirit, carve a smile
As you flip through these pages,
Sharing the many sentiments of women . . .
I hope in the end . . .
You find it all worthwhile! . . .

You feel loved . . . .
Inspired in being a woman . . . .
Loving LIFE!

Laarni Manalac-Fajardo

To Flor . . . .

Pen . . . .

and all the B's . . . .

with all my love,

Laarni

An Ode

to

Women

AN ODE TO WOMEN

A Woman's BEAUTY . . .
So enchanting, alluring,
Her smile . . .
Captivating, deceiving . . .
Her eyes . . . impressive
Talking to you . . .
Touching your heart . . .
Embracing you!

A woman's passion
And hunger for LOVE . . .
Unfathomable,
Without measure . . .
Knows no time nor age
In a lifetime . . .
In abundance overflowing,
Engulfing . . . consuming!

A woman's TEARS shed
in the silence of her heart . . .
hiding within,
a strength . . .
beneath her gentleness
and body that seems delicate . . .
lies much endurance, perseverance
and patience!

A woman's WISDOM is so profound
Far deeper than what you can see through her eyes . . .
Her understanding prevails
When things are far from being understood,
With her heart discerning . . .
against all odds . . . all knowing,
learnt from being loved . . . being hurt,
. . . from LOVE itself!

A woman with her ethereal ESSENCE . . .
Character and many sentiments,
Embodies that someone
Special in our lives . . .
Sharing, touching
Loving all that we are!

3

Rainbows of my Life

RAINBOWS OF MY LIFE

RED . . . *colors my world with love*
Embracing, cuddling me with warmth . . .
From friends, loved ones and the like
. . . may it be from the past or now . . . .

ORANGE . . . *envelops me with much passion*
In things that I do with my heart
Working with zest, giving all my best . . .
Expecting nothing . . . in return! . . . .

I'm bursting in **YELLOW** . . . *with all my joy*
With everythin' I could hardly fathom
The smiles, laughter, and wonderful moments
All for me . . . to treasure forever!

Yet **BLUE** . . . *at times sinks within me*
In melancholy, creeping through my veins,
Everytime I'm hurt . . . cast away in pain . . .
Frustrations, disappointments . . .
All too hard to decipher . . .
sometimes things . . . are just not fair! . . .

But then again **GREEN** *. . . jumps up on me*
  Awakening me with much hope . . .
Compelling me to heed for tomorrow
  Leaving the past and to look back . . . Not! . . .

INDIGO *. . . comes as life's full of surprises*
  Concealed behind that silhouette . . .
Grasp it, take it with full hands . . .
  Seize it, make the most of it . . .
    . . . and make it all worthwhile! . . .

VIOLET *. . . reflects my fervent faith*
  In whatever life awaits me . . .
My world may shatter but it will not wither . . .
  The serenity and peace . . .
    That HE fills me with!

Love

LOVE

Love with its dawn . . . sunset
And varying hues . . .
This heart of mine,
You gently imprisons and woos . . .
As a beckoning star
In an enchanting night . . .
Summoning my emotions . . . to light . . . .

Love can play wonder
And make me smile . . .
Uplift my spirit . . .
With laughter and delight!
Command my feet
And dance with frolic and glee . . .
Embracing joy . . . you . . . ME!

Yet love is a key . . .
That can secretly unlock
The fortress within you
And break your heart . . .
Weakening . . . blinding . . .
Chain you with strong hands . . .
Leaving you hurt . . . torn . . . and numb!

Love may bring back
The hands of time . . .
Love may bring forth
New beginnings . . .
Love always will be
A part of my life . . .
A song forever . . .
Playing in my heart!

Unrequited Love

WILL I EVER LOVE AGAIN?

It's not the footsteps as you walked out that door
Nor the so many apologies that you've made before
That weigh heavily in my heart . . .
It's the truth you're walkin' out of my life . . . .

It's not the silence deafening this room
Nor the echo as you said your goodbye all too soon
That keeps on resounding in my head . . .
It's the emptiness you carved in my heart in the end . . . .

Loving you then . . . .
Loving you still . . .
How will my heart ever love again?
I kept on believin' there was us
Now it's gone . . .
All gone with the past . . . .

Will I ever see tomorrow?
Will I ever see light?
When all I can see is myself . . .
in streamin' tears . . . being drowned!

Loving you then . . .
Loving you still . . .
Tell me, will I ever love again?

DISILLUSIONED

I thought there was us
After all this time
But it was just me
Make believing all the while . . . .
You kept me waiting for tomorrows
which never came . . .
And left me with those
Broken promises that you made . . .

Did you ever love me?
Did you ever care?
Did you ever think . . .
I'll forever be chained . . .
to your playful heart . . .
Insensitive . . . stoned
Leavin' me numbed . . .
Broken and torn!

I ask you now . . . Do you feel alright?
Can you still look me in the eye?
Is this the kind of love . . . you said was real?
It was for me . . . but I'm disillusioned now!

Why does it have to end this way . . .
I love you still . . . It isn't fair!

AWAY FROM YOU

It seems like forever, I was livin' a lie
Believing there was us . . . all this time . . .
But I'm finally awake now . . . that everything's gone . . .
It's time to move on and tell myself to be strong . . .

Walk away from you . . . far from you
Erase you from my world . . .
And tell myself, no more us . . .
It's finally the end!

No more living in your shadows
It's time for me to be free
No more pretending that I need you
It's time for me to love . . . ME!

Away from you . . .
With no turning back . . .
far from you . . .
Leaving the past behind!

STILL

It's been quite a long time
That I've forgotten how you smiled . . .
But with you standing in front of me
You still have that look in your eye!

For a minute, I was lost for words
Didn't know what to say or do . . .
In such a haste, it brought me back
To the time when there was you!

Why do our paths need to cross now?
Is it fate that brought you back?
But after all that's changed and happened . . .
Don't you think . . .
it's a little bit too late now?

Yet one thing still remains,
to you, I must admit,
My feelings for you then . . .
For some reason is unchanged!

Likewise this one question
Forever resonating in my head . . .
Which all this time you left unanswered . . .
"Did you ever love me then?"

Loved

I LOVE YOU

You came to my life gently
And I couldn't say a word
You looked me in the eye . . .
And right there . . . YOU were the one!

I tried to look away
Afraid not of you but me
Trying so hard not to fall . . .
But I wasn't strong enough after all!

In so short a time I've fallen
But I don't regret it, not a bit
For with you I found a love that is . . .
True and all . . . and complete!

Moments spent with you
And time stands still
And when we are apart . . .
My heart's beatin' for you still!

You always find the rhymes to all of my songs
The will, the strength for me to carry on
And if I have to say one last from my heart
. . . I simply love you . . . all my life!

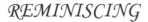

REMINISCING

It's been awhile now
Since we said our goodbyes
Away from you . . .
Away from my love . . .

But the memories live on
Of happy moments
With you . . . in your embrace
And tender loving ways . . .

With a smile in my heart
Here I am reminiscing
Our togetherness, our laughter
sharing, loving . . . special days!

Every moment with you then
And time stood still . . .
But now away from you
In my heart, it is still you I feel . . .

Time soon flies so swift
And we'll be in each others' arms again
For us to weave our dreams together
You and I as one . . .
United by our love . . .
And tomorrow will be ours! . . . .

THE DAY I SAID I DO

I cherish this special day
With you . . .
We've decided to tie the knot
And say I DO . . . .

Leavin my old self,
single and carefree
Embracing
the world . . . of you & me . . .

I wear this dress
Simple & white
My heart racing, overwhelmed . . .

I walk the aisle
With fingers clasped
Holdin a bouquet of flowers . . .

It seems all a dream . . .
While our song being sang
Feeling the warmth from family & friends
Seeing the smiles in their eyes . . . .

With every single breath I take
I come to you, step by step
As dad handed me to you
tears of joy . . . I shed

At the altar, we exchanged vows
And God's blessings we received
Behold my husband! . . . I thee wed
our love sealed with a kiss!

As man & wife in hand
No longer me nor you alone . . .
But "US" as ONE . . . .
From this day on!

I'M YOURS . . . FAITHFULLY

A lot of things are before us now
But it gets a lot more special . . .
It still overwhelms me being with you . . .
. . . and that's for a lifetime!

Each passing day . . . we come to know each other
As new things unfold before us
I'm glad to share all them with you . . .
no matter what . . . I shall stay true!

Things in the past, another year gone,
But through it all . . . love was always in our hearts!
Your presence in my life truly makes me happy
I ask nothing more . . . you complete me!

But let me just say . . .
I love you . . .
More than words can say . . .
More than you'll ever know!

Thank you so much for everything . . .
For being you . . .
For letting me be
For loving me . . .
I'm yours . . . Faithfully!

MUSING

Here I am at work
Looking at these paper works . . .
Yet my thoughts are flying . . .
Flying out to you . . .

My heart longing just for you
It's always been you . . . all along
And now it excites me even more
Now a baby . . . is in my womb . . .

I wonder if he's a he or a she
Will he look like you or me
Will he have eyes like yours, my love
Or have your smile which captured my heart? . . .

What name shall we give him
Will I be a good mom? . . .
Oh I have so many questions in my mind
I know the answer . . . in time, we'll find . . .

For now, as I've always said
I really do appreciate . . .
Every little thing you do
With all my love . . . I do thank you!

Your patience, understanding and love
For me . . . are more than enough . . .
I hope I'm making you happy just the same
I love you . . . till the end!

WIVES' WHISPERS

I waited for this day
Which you have forgotten yet again . . .
Well, it's nothin' special really,
It's just our anniversary . . . .

You promised this time you'll make it . . .
But you we're caught in a meeting or traffic?
It's nothin' really big . . .
It's just our kid's show you've missed . . .

You always seems to forget things
Or hardly notice anything . . .
Straight from work, you grab the paper . . .
While our child into a lady is growing . . .

You have this special "time warp"
When you immerse yourself in this world . . .
Of gym, cars and football,
Ipad, golf, playstations . . .

I thought you'll give me a hand
In rearing up our child . . .
but all you did was leave me . . .
with all these sleepless nights . . .

The night growing deeper,
The kids now all in bed . . .
And here I am waiting,
As you are still out with friends . . .

You said you'll find a decent job
Which you've uttered a thousand times . . .
Yet you spent another day at home . . .
As I arrived from work at four . . .

I'm really not used to working,
Doin' a full time job . . .
But here I am juggling . . .
Work and family life . . .

And there you go again,
When things go out of hand . . .
Losing your temper, raising your voice . . .
Uttering words I've heard before . . .

We have our petty quarrels,
These silly arguments . . . .
And here I am crying,
Emotional, sensitive . . . hurting . . . .

Yet as the day kisses its sunset
I go to bed disheartened not . . .
knowing as I greet the dawn . . .
I'm still your wife . . . for life!

Amidst all the reasons in my eyes,
That sometimes makes you seem to fade . . .
Faithful as your wife, I remain . . .
Understanding . . .
Believing . . .
LOVING!

ALL MY LIFE

You know we can always go & explore
Do nothing at all or something more
I sing your song, you do my dance
We share our dreams, fears, tears & smiles . . .

Verses & rhymes, I can write you loads
But none of them can ever come close
To what my heart wants to capture & say
For who you are & your special ways . . .

The love, gratitude, joy & pride
Of simply havin' you in my life
An amazing father to our little ones
A loving husband to your dear wife . . .

Through life's ups & downs, I see tomorrow with YOU
May it be bright or bleak, I'll greet each dawn a-new
So this I say with a tear in my eye,
In my breath a sigh, in my heart a smile . . .
I love you all my life . . .
I thank GOD for giving me YOU . . .
And to you . . . I'll always say . . ." I DO!"

Love
of a
Mother

LONGING

Months, weeks, days . . .
How time has flown
Counting each passing night
Waiting for each coming dawn

When can I touch you
Finally come to see you . . .
Hold you in my arms
As I feel you close to my heart?

Each move that you make
In my womb makes me smile . . . .
Wondering what you might be doing
Do you stretch . . . do you glide?

Each morn as I awake
My excitement just grows stronger . . .
When will you ever come
Out to this world, I wonder?

MY PRECIOUS ONE

Alas! The long wait is over
"Welcome to the world!"
Our hearts overwhelmed with joy
Anxieties and worries . . . gone!

As I held you in my arms
As I feel your skin next to mine . . .
Tears fell from my eyes
Gazing at you . . . I gave a sigh!

What a wonderful gift you are
Sent from heaven's above . . .
You're one sweet little angel
With all our love . . . to cuddle!

The Lord indeed is good
For you are an amazing grace . . .
Our hearts are filled with gratitude
In just so many ways!

MY PRINCESS' FIRST YEAR

At **1** month . . . you talked to us through your eyes
And we caressed you with our love and touch

At **2** months . . . you were christened
Right on daddy's birthday

At **3** months . . . you've given us your 1st lovely smile
And rolling over, you did try

At **4** months . . . you had your 1st baby food
And "dada" happens to be your 1st word

At **5** months . . . you've done your 1st "Trick or Treat"
With 4 other kids down the street

At **6** months . . . you tried to pull yourself up
And experienced your 1st Christmas time!

At **7** months . . . . you started to walk with support
And you did enjoy your 1st fall of "snow"!

At **8** months . . . your 1st tiny tooth has shown
And you are now trying to stand on your own

At **9** months . . . you're crawling and likewise "sit"
And can manage to do a couple of steps!

At **10** months . . . you started to walk on your own
And watchin' the telly . . . you enjoy

At **11** months . . . mommy has weaned you off from
breastfeeding
Formula and baby foods . . . you're happy with!

And finally now that YOU are **ONE** . . .
You've come to visit our lovely "hometown" . . .
Everyone said . . ." You're simply the "darling" of the crowd!
And truly a "blessing" . . . from above!

MY LITTLE BOY'S MILESTONES

At **1** month . . . with your big and black round eyes
So expressive for always, it sure talked to us

At **2** months . . . you had your first Christmas time
And you were amazed with all the Christmas lights!

At **3** months . . . you began showing us your smile
So charming, it truly melted our hearts

At **4** months . . . you started to make this "coo"
As sister Amie plays "peek-a-boo" on you

At **5** months . . . you were christened
At this Catholic Church, on a Monday . . .
Mommy's family from abroad came to visit
To give you a cuddle and they were delighted!

At **6** months . . . you had your 1st baby food
And "mama" happens to be your 1st word

*At **7** months . . . it's like you wanted to do everything*
From rolling over, crawling, sitting & standing

*At **8** months . . . your 1ˢᵗ tiny tooth came out*
And you can giggle and really laugh out loud!

*At **9** months . . . you've tried to stand on your own*
And looking at books with sounds, you enjoy

*At **10** months . . . you started walking on your own*
Following "sis", wherever she goes . . .

*At **11** months . . . you're truly all over the house*
Even climb up the stairs, you can do so now!

*And finally now, that you are **ONE** . . .*
You're our little BIG BOY, with these 12 months gone
You're truly a "blessing" from above
With the JOY that you give . . . to all of US! ☺

THE KIDS' DAYS AT NURSERY

Time indeed has flown so fast
Now it's time to say goodbye
But I know you'll leave with a smile ☺
For indeed, it's been all worthwhile!

Your days at Nursery have always been fun
For all you've seen and done
From starting to pray . . . to tidying up
you've truly learned a lot!

Singing, dancing, playing outside
Doing some baking and dressing up
painting, coloring, drawing too
all these you loved . . . you really do!

Artwork, computer, playing with dough
And lovely stories you listened to
Doodling, counting, telling the time
All these and more sure made you smile!

And you shall not forget "special days"...
Definitely not the "thinking chair"
Like your visit to the library
And your field trip, you see!

Not to mention all your friends
Whom you have enjoyed playing with
And your lovely teachers who have always been nice
With their happy faces and lovely smiles!

So to all your teachers,
Our simple "Thank you" comes their way
For doing a brilliant job
May God bless their hearts! ☺

I'M WEARING A TUTU

Another day with you my little ones
I wonder what shall we do this time . . .

Play with puzzles or Snakes & Ladders
Play with cars or your make-believe house?
Watch a video with all your cuddly toys? . . .
What about some sing-along
Which you always enjoy?

Or shall we do some artwork
With your crayons and stickers . . .
Let's do some drawing . . .
With your colored pens? . . .

Or shall we jump
And roll in bed . . .
Simply play "tickle" . . . ?
Oh! I just love your giggles!

Or do you want mommy
To do her magic tricks . . .
Which you never get tired of
And always leaves you amazed?

What about playin' pretend
With your favorite tea set . . .
I'll do the ordering
While you do the cooking? . . .

Or maybe we better make it real
And bake some yummy cupcakes . . .
We'll mix the batter
Then you lick the spoon after!

Or maybe you want to go outside
In your playhouse . . .
Or whiz around in your bikes?
We can play "tag"
which always tires me out . . .
Or maybe just chill
on the swing while we sing? . . .

Think . . . think . . .
And here you two come . . .
One as a princess . . . .
One as a fireman!

With your cheeky smiles
You hand me these . . .
A fairy wing and a tutu . . .
So "dressing up" . . . it is!

We had a lovely time
As we usually do . . .
And before goin' to bed . . .
I read you a book . . . .

We prayed afterwards
Then I kiss you goodnight . . .
With a tear and a smile . . .
Hiding a fear in my heart . . . .

My precious little ones
I know time will come . . .
You'll soon get tired
Of playing with mom . . .

But I'll always remember . . .
I will sure do . . .
All the times I washed the dishes . . .
"wearing a tutu" . . . .

I LOVE YOU, MY CHILD

I was distraught
Looking back . . .
On the past
That we both had . . .
you were barely 3 then
so innocent . . .
I wished I could protect you . . .
But that time . . .
I just couldn't . . .

With the time fleeting by . . .
I buried my heart with work
Striving, struggling,
Pretending I've got strength . . .

I worked and worked
Without giving up . . .
Givin' my all . . .
All that I have . . .

My life's without meaning
Without you in it . . .
You give me direction,
You keep me going . . .

But looking at you now
After all this time . . .
Sometimes I can't bear ignoring
The pain hiding in your eyes . . . .

It's you and me
Against the world,
I'd like you to understand
I am here standing . . .
For you . . . no matter what!

With God's steadfast love
Embracin' both of us . . .
I love you my child . . .
Your life's more precious
Than mine! . . .

TREASURES IN MY HEART

Your pitter patter feet,
Tiny, little hands trying to reach . . .
Me, wipin' your tears,
Kissin' away your fears . . .
Our silly quiet times,
Singing nursery rhymes . . .
Your laughter and giggles,
Your whispers to my ears . . .

Wavin' goodbye,
On the day I sent you to school for the first time . . .
Us . . . sharin' everything,
Even the littlest things . . . .
Splashes in the bath,
Playin' with shadows in the dark . . .
Pullin' funny faces,
Icing on our noses . . . .

Our summer holidays,
All special in so many ways . . .
Our walks in the sand, stroll in the park,
Flyin' a kite, your first horseback ride . . .
Your warm little hugs,
Your ever charming smiles . . .
Your sweet voice saying . . .
"I love you, mom!" . . . .

All these are my precious
Little treasures in my heart . . .
I'll always cherish in memory,
As time flying by . . . .

For now you're a fine young wo/man,
Like sand, slipping through my hands . . .
Drifting away gently,
As you go through life . . . .

But nothing will ever change,
Amidst my wrinkles and gray hair . . .
You'll always be mom's little one . . .
Much LOVED . . . then and now!

FAMILY

F— amily is where I find **JOY** in my heart . . .

A— beckoning STAR . . .
that lifts me up and inspires,
with

M—emories so special . . .
unfolding through **TIME** . . .

I— nterlacing moments of then and **NOW** . . .

L— ance, Amie and Mark, thou art **MINE,**

Y— ou are my **LOVE**, my **LIFE** . . .
for all **TIME!**

Career

NURSES

N—urses are not just those in uniforms and caps
Running around for errands . . .
They are simple persons with such BIG hearts
holding your hands . . . making you smile!

U—nequalled are their passion . . .
For their chosen work,
Their commitment and pride . . .
Are simply beyond words!

R—emarkable are they . . .
Carrying on with their shifts
Hiding the tiredness . . .
Walking on those feet!

S—pecial are their ways . . .
Supportive advocates
Bringing out the best . . .
For their patients!

E—ver dedicated . . .
With their gentle hands . . .
Warming your hearts . . .
. . . touching lives!

A TEACHER'S VOICE

It's late in the evening
But I'm still up . . .
Burying my head
Working on lesson plans . . .

Tomorrow by six
I should be rushin' to work . . .
Managin' to grab
Just a mug of hot drink!

I feel so tired,
exhausted, worn out
Yet as I step in school,
I feel all revitalized . . .

Cheerful greetings from the students,
With their grin and happy smiles . . .
Their sweet simple gestures . . .
Makin' me feel appreciated and loved!

A few times now
I've lost my voice . . .
But I try with my patience . . . not!
Knowin' that learning . . .
Do take time!

Trying my best
To impart, to share . . .
Whatever I know . . .
To make them grow!

I always remember
As their second parent,
With values & discipline . . .
In their minds to inculcate!

Be there to support
And likewise to guide them . . .
Be there to listen
And be a friend!

As a teacher,
These things, I keep in mind
Rememberin' sometime ago . . .
I was too a student once!

As a teacher
I take joy and pride . . .
Molding something great
Through time . . . from simple little minds!

I AM A CAREER-WOMAN

I may be an office-worker,
An entrepreneur,
A banker, teacher
designer, manager . . . .

Yes! I am single
And happy as I am,
Not tied to anyone . . .
I am a career-woman!

I make my own decisions
And I am strong-willed . . .
I firmly believe
"I'm the master of my own fate"!

But don't be mistaken . . .
Deep inside I maybe weak,
Feeling at a lost . . .
Not knowing where to go!

I am single . . .
Though I did love before,
It's just that things
Didn't work at all!

I am not bitter . . .
Told myself not to be,
Rememberin' a friend
Who once said to me . . .

"She who for love has undergone
The worst that can befall,
Is happier a thousandfold than one . . .
Who never loved . . . at all!"

If love does knock
At my door like before . . .
Will I welcome it or not.? . . .
We'll never know . . .

But as of now I am single
As I choose to be . . .
Feelin' the love
From friends and family!

I'm a career-woman
And I am happy with who I am . . .
Loving life . . .
being . . . a woman!

AS YOUR CARER

Your mental, physical health
Leaving you in need of help . . .
Which called for me
To have this commitment . . .

In supporting, assisting you
be there for you to guide . . .
amidst all circumstances . . .
to LOVE!

Prepare your day,
Show you the way . . .
Share your fears and smiles . . .
Share your sunrise,
Kiss the stars goodnight . . .
Be your ears, be your eyes . . .
Be there for you . . .
For LIFE!

With patience and understanding,
Give you a hand . . .
Even though it becomes
Difficult at times . . . .

Amidst the worries,
Thinking of you . . .
For all the times,
For a moment to leave you,

For all the disappointments,
Tears I shed . . .
For all the times,
I felt helpless myself!

As your CARER . . .
I made this commitment,
I told myself
For mine to KEEP . . .

Amidst all odds,
Getting strength from God . . .
From people around,
That gives hope in my HEART!

Embracing each day,
Come what may . . . .
Feeling that sense of JOY . . .
In getting you through life and . . . ALL!

MY MENTOR

Here I am hoping to learn
Needing all the support I can get . . .
In my studies or at work
And here you are . . . ready to help!

With your smile
And look in your eyes . . .
I know right then
I'll be OK . . .

The way you talk
And share your views . . .
The things you say,
Special in so many ways!

Encouraging, inspiring,
Motivating, nurturing . . .
That's why
I look up to you!

You walk the talk,
Things that you taught . . .
That simply makes me
Want to be like you!

As my mentor,
You're one of a kind . . .
In all you say and do!

A role model
And likewise a friend,
So from my heart . . .
I do THANK you! ☺

I'M NO PLAIN HOUSEWIFE

It's 6 o' clock, and the alarm goes
But I'm still havin' a snore . . .
In my dressin' gown
I walk down the stairs . . .
Half awake,
Without combin' my hair . . .

I prepare your breakfast,
Scrambled egg on toast . . .
And your coffee,
As you like it . . .
Freshly brewed!

I prepare all your clothes
Which I've ironed last night . . .
Then I set the table
While all of you take a bath!

I kiss you goodbye
While I bring the kids to school . . .
Then come back home
To do the household chores!

Cleaning the house
While havin' some music . . .
Doin' the dishes
While the washing is running!

In the afternoon
I do some shoppin'...
Maybe after
I had some pamperin'....

May it be in the spa
Or gym for my aerobics
or to the salon...
to have my nails painted!

3 o' clock...
Time to pick up the kids
Then crack my head helpin' them...
with their homework....

By 6pm,
I have to cook supper
Before you arrive...
Around half past seven!

After eating...
I put the kids to bed,
Read them a book
And pray afterwards...

Between 9 and 10...
With a smile,
I kiss you goodnight...
Sayin' to myself,
"I'm no plain housewife"!

I love what I'm doin'
It's my FULL TIME JOB...
I feel much fulfilled...
As a mother and wife!

AWAY FROM HOME

Here we are in a land that's foreign
Miles away from home
Embracin' its culture, speaking its tongue
Making its world . . . as our own!

With its fast paced clock
We're ever tryin' to keep up
Abidin' by its rules, we do . . .

Walkin' through its fields
To most of us, it may seem . . .
Is truly but a dream . . . come true!

But nevertheless,
despite the change in air
We now breathe and colors that we see . . .

I firmly believe, our hearts still lies
Where it truly belongs . . . and yearns to be!

With family and friends
Faith and values we've kept
And loved through all these years . . .

Nothin' compares to "Home Sweet Home"
. . . with every sunset and
. . . each comin' dawn!

Family I Grew Up With

GRANDMA

To you . . . our one and only grandma,
A glorious birthday greetings do we give . . .
On the 80th year that marks your birth,
That we are joyfully celebrating!

Looking back in our childhood days . . .
You've always been present guiding,
May it be in difficulties or joy . . .
You were with us . . . through them all!

With all this passing time
A lot of changes might have happened . . .
But all your loving memories . . .
In our hearts, will never be erased!

From your children, grandchildren
And great-grandchildren . . .
We are all here loving you . . .

With all our THANKS and heart-felt prayer,
That a much longer life . . .
Our Lord will grant YOU!

MOTHER

You simply exudes beauty . . .
as a dainty F lower in bloom
Remindin us that L ife . . .
in itself, . . . is beautiful!

You're the gentle mo O n
looking down on us . . .
With your R adiant light guiding . . .
when we're lost in the D ark . . . .

You're a ray of glorious sunshin E
Giving us warmth . . .
Comforting, reassuring
L ovingly embracing us . . . .

You're a refreshing t I ny raindrop
Revitali Z ing . . . offering hope . . .
so the dishearthened heart within us . . .
could take he A rt again . . . once more!

IN MEMORY OF MAMA

It seems only yesterday
I still can hear your voice
You're ever soft-spoken,
Mild-mannered . . .
A lady so prim & proper . . . .

I can't remember you being cross,
Nor ever raising your voice . . .
But I remember your gentle singing
And words of endearment whenever you're calling . . .
(Brother was Darling and I was Love,
My two other sisters . . .
Sweetheart and Child!)

Once I chanced upon some notes you've written
Words of love to Papa which kept me thinkin'
It must be from you then I got this inkling
on verses & rhymes . . . and all my writing . . .

You're exceptionally brilliant in needlework
the likes of crocheting & sawing
and you have this hook you make use of
to make a rug or mat of sort . . . .

Curtains, tablecloths,
uniforms, our clothes
Special & beautiful,
You patiently made them all . . .

I miss our walks to the market
with you never failing to buy my faves
like Funny comics & loads of songhits . . .
all these silly, simple things . . .

I miss the smile on your face on every school event
family days, Field demos, liturgical concerts
or that time when I first composed my poem . . .
You were with Papa to share my joy . . .

You're ever gentle & kind in all your ways
You've taught us fine values
and all about faith . . .

All the early mornings you woke up
preparing us for school . . .
Now I ask myself . . . .
"Have we loved you enough . . . after all?"

15 years of knowin' you may not been long
but it's enough for me to forever sing your song . . .
Your song of love & dedication
as a mother & a wife . . .
Your memory lingers on . . .
in our hearts . . . in our lives . . .

A woman that's fair skinned
with curly short hair . . .
chinky eyes & heartwarming smile . . .

A lady of yellow, with gentle touch
with a heart full of love . . .
Simply beautiful inside & out!

PAPA'S 60TH

What can we do to make you feel
The pride, the love we hold within?
For all you've done, for all you've been . . .
For all you are, all through these years?

Build you a monument, write you a song?
Make a poem or two?
But all these things, nothing compares . . .
When it comes to knowing . . . "YOU"!

We've come to appreciate the beauty of life
Because of your example
The pains, the hardships . . . one has to strive
To taste the sweet fruits of labor!

The sincere, humble person in you
Helpful and faithful too . . .
The values you uphold, all through this time
Have been pillars of strength in our minds!

It must have not been easy for you
To let us realize these things before
But now we've got families of our own . . .
We promise, to our children . . . we'll pass them on!

And now it is your 60th,
We wish you Papa . . ." more of life"
And as you have always said . . .
we know, for you . . . ." GOD WILL PROVIDE"!

A SALUTE TO YOU DAD

A Salute to you dad
From our hearts do we give . . .
For the things that you've done
And to all you have been!

A father like you
Is truly a rare gem . . .
With honor and pride
You give to our name!

A Salute to you dad
Is but a simple gesture . . .
For countless deed you've done
Which time couldn't measure!

Someone like YOU
With a sincere, kind heart
Humble and faithful
With such generous hands!

A Salute to you dad
For all these years . . .
Of hardships and labor
You painstakingly take!

A person like you
With values you uphold . . .
Dedication and commitment
To your family and all!

A Salute to you dad
For the person that you are
Whom the good Lord has given
To others and to us!

May the Lord bless and keep you
As you walk each day of your life
And always remember dad . . .
We love you with a grateful heart! ☺

MY DEAR SISTER

How far should I look back
To recall when we were little
Innocent, carefree playin'
Out in the sun or when it's rainin' . . . .

Doin' silly things together
That will mostly end in quarrels
We just never get tired doin'
Yet forgettin' why it started . . . .

Through our growin' up years
At one point, it crossed my mind
Sis, are we growin' apart,
'coz it's like were heading separate lives . . . .

But then again, the way we are now
I guess I was mistaken . . .
Though physically we are apart
The distance between us . . . I think not!

For how ironic, this I feel
You're much closer to me . . . it's surreal
All this time, God has kept us together
Amidst changing seasons, time and weather!

Pouring our hearts out
Sharing the ups & downs of life
You're now a fine woman,
A mother and a wife . . .

Yet over the phone, listening to your voice
I still can see the innocent you . . .
My dear younger sister . . . my best friend . . . .
I'm here for you & will always love you! ☺

TO YOU BROTHER

Where has the time gone?, I ask
It seems only yesterday . . .
I was sixteen, you were seven
But look at you now . . . a family man!

Away from your son & lovely wife
Sailing the deep vast sea
Away from home where your heart lies
And where you'd rather be . . .

I see this truth every time . . .
I get to see you in the eye
In all our precious rendezvous
In all your ports or right in my home . . .

I see the pain in your smiles
Which you always try to hide
I feel the hardships that you take
Whenever I give you a hug . . . .

But this you should remember
We're ever proud of you
With all the endeavors that you take
We pray to the Lord to guide you . . . .

And I have this fervent prayer
That may you find your heart's content
You'll need not sail the vast sea again
And be with your son & wife, instead!

We may not have a lot in common
And we may have a great age gap
But you'll always be my dear brother
Who's got a special place in my heart!

Childhood
Memories

ALMA MATER

11 fruitful years . . .
From Prep to Highschool,
I was taught and nurtured
At this Catholic school . . .

Exclusive for girls
Run by the FMM (Franciscan Missionaries of Mary) . . .
Who inculcated in our minds the words . . .
"Ad Veritatem, Per Caritatem"!
(To Truth, Through Charity)

Enriched with such
unforgettable moments
Shared by wonderful
teachers and friends . . . .

Such sweet memories
I hold dear in my heart
mine to treasure & cherish . . .
with immeasurable joy & pride!

STELLANS

S— tellans are made of wonderful girls

T— alented, witty & special in their ways . . .

E— ver beautiful inside & out

L— ovely and charming with their smiles

without a doubt

L— iving a life in faith, hope & love

A— ll that's learnt from knowing GOD . . .

N— ever forgettin' the values taught

HAIL STELLA MARIS! . . .

S— o proud . . . with all!

CHRISTMAS REUNIONS

Cold, chilly mornings,
Tiny bells tinkling,
Jolly spirit in the air . . .
Your heart singing . . .

Loads of smiles and laughing,
Many warm hugs—giving,
Cheerful songs everywhere . . .
It's Christmas time again!

Busy with your shopping,
Lookin' forward to gift-giving,
Feasting on sumptuous food . . .
fun and games . . . all so good!

Families from the city . . .
Going out in the country,
Meeting up with the clan . . .
All giving love to gran!

Looking at aunts and uncles . . .
Who seem not to change at all
While cousins, nieces and nephews . . .
All seem to be bigger than before!

Being the eldest amongst cousins,
You remember hosting the party . . .
Doin' all the games
Oh how you enjoyed it!

Starting with thanksgiving . . .
All ending with much loving,
You'll be looking forward again . . .
To next year's Christmas day!

Reunions will always be special,
Creating lovely memories in my heart . . .
May God bless our families . . .
through the passing time!

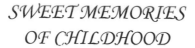

SWEET MEMORIES
OF CHILDHOOD

Childhood memories indeed flies me back
Home with nostalgia when youth was in my grasp
Innocence embraces me, time then was my friend
Laughter encircles my world without end!

Doing what the young ones do now . . . a far cry from my
past
Having many hi tech games and toys that don't last
Occupied was I then with simple things amongst friends
Out in the streets, under a tree . . . oh how we played with
such glee!

Days and years have flown so swift and gone are those lovely
times
When the sun touched our faces and the moon smiled on
us
We were agile and strong, naively frolicked outdoors
Not tied to computers, mobiles, all those sorts!

We didn't have much funfares or amusement parks
Yet we're happy and contented, with what we had
With all the excitement when the rain pours down
Then chasing after rainbows, when it is all done!

We didn't have enough sweeties or chocolates, I shall say
Or went on holidays as much as whenever you now may
Yet we enjoyed and was amused, with an ice cream in our hand
Strolling along the riverside, oh that was pure delight!

Not much was expected of us during my time
Like doing so many things on your own . . . at the age of five
We were carefree, light hearted as fleeting wind, you see
Yet we knew our limitations and we were happy as can be!

We always had time to go to Sunday mass
And spent some quiet family times
Time then was not at all fast-paced
As it is now, in surmountable ways!

The values I was taught, by my parents were so poignant
Inculcated in my mind, amidst time passing by
But like drifting sand in my palms,
they must have been gone
Amongst now's generation . . .
with so many things in their minds!

There was more interaction, I shall say "personal" touch
  amongst family and friends, I hold dear in my heart
Happiness you can reach without so much expense
  Life indeed was simpler yet beautiful . . . then!

If only I could turn back the hands of time
  And fly me to the spring of my youth . . . 'twas mine
Once more, let me touch my world in varying hues
  Allow me to dance to the sweet music too!

For as I walk the stream of life . . .
  reminiscing all of these
As it warms my heart, paints a smile on my face . . .
  I cherish all these memories

As I close my eyes in silence . . .
  once more it becomes vivid and alive
My happy days . . . I shall find . . . .
  In my childhood days . . . where it truly lies!

Friends

FRIENDS . . .
SISTERS BY HEART!

We've shared our deepest secrets
No one else supposed to know
We've shared the love we had . . .
Gone . . . forgotten long ago . . . .

We've shared our tears in silence
We endlessly then shed
We've shared our broken hearts
Which then completely bled . . . .

We've shared each joy in our hands . . .
Triumphs and successes
We've shared a thousand laughter . . .
Smiles and happiness . . .

We've shared our hopes, dreams and wishes
For what the future holds
We've shared the past and yesterday
And what we can reminiscence at all . . .

And yet with the passing time
That brought us to what is now . . .
We still continue to share the "US"
Of what is in our lives . . .

We know each others 'weaknesses
We've seen each others' worst . . .
Yet amidst all of these
We accept one another . . . just the same . . . .

To this, I say . . . "I treasure you!"
You're a blessing without a doubt . . . .
I really do think and feel as friends . . .
. . . we're truly sisters by heart! ☺

NO GOODBYES

Time indeed has flown so swift
For now, is it time to say goodbye?
But let's not fret, we need not weep . . .
For we've got mem'ries . . . for us to keep!

We truly had such fun and laughter
Special moments . . . we'll treasure forever
And as we remember and we look back
They shall create . . . smiles in our hearts!

But I'll not say "Farewell" to you
For it's not yet "goodbye" . . . it's true!
Instead, I'll say . . ." Thank you very much!"
For everything . . . this comes from my heart!

Till then, "Good Luck" and take care
My dearly beloved friends
Hoping too for "All the Best!"
For us all and May God Bless!

These heartfelt words I send to you
With all my love . . . I really do
With the thought that soon one day
We'll be together . . . once again!

Interests

THE POEM

The poem . . .
in my young mind
I've written . . .

Lost in time
but never forgotten . . .

my innocence then
awakened . . .

Must have inspired me
with my pen and paper . . .

to carry on
with all my writings . . .

'Twas a long time ago . . .

My first ever poem . . .
which started it all!

MY LOVE OF MUSIC

I've always loved songs . . .
With its melody and rhythm,
Its lyrics and rhymes . . .
All so captivating!

I have always loved music
And the feelings
it brings . . .
I likewise play the piano . . .
And appreciated
concerts that I've been!

I've enjoyed being part
Of singing groups
and of choirs . . .
And actually had a gig
with a band . . .
Once upon a time!

I'm not really a brilliant singer . . .
Let's just say . . .
"I sing from the heart!"
With my singing . . .
I do feel free,
As songs touch my heart . . .
Taking a hold of me!

Songs indeed can travel
you back in time
Bringing back memories
of people to life . . .

I delight in sharing
the songs in my heart . . .
Siging the "person" . . .
that I am . . . through time!

Blessings . . . How Do I Count Thee?

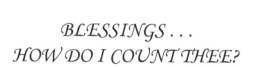

BLESSINGS...
HOW DO I COUNT THEE?

As I stepped out in the garden
And breathe the crisp morning
With a cup of freshly brewed coffee . . .
Oh! It's heaven embracin'!

Lovely azure on high
Fluffy white clouds floating by
Glorious sunshine greeting . . .
Little birds chirping . . .

Green lush grass carpet
A burst of colors scattered
Gorgeous sweet scent . . .
From an array of beautiful flowers!

Butterflies fluttering by
Bees buzzing around
Soft tinkling of the chimes
Swayin with the whispering wind . . .
My dainty friendly fairies . . .
Dancing with their wings!

Sparkling rainwater
Filling the shallow birdbath
Fresh morning dew touching . . .
the leaves and velvet petals!

The rainbow painting the sky,
Creating a glistening prism . . .
Me, walking out in the fields . . .
Listening to the rustling of the leaves!

Gazing at the majestic waterfalls,
While crossing a running brook . . .
Stepping on stones,
Up in a hill . . .
Singing my song!

Serene deep blue seas,
Gentle waves kissing the shore . . .
Sands caressing my feet . . .
Gently tickling my toes!

Star studded skies
With the shimmering moonlight . . .
My kids tucked in bed . . .
Kissing them goodnight!

Trials in my way,
Tears that I shed . . .
Things that made me falter
Yet made me stronger . . . in the end!

Triumphs in my heart,
My unwavering faith in God . . .
Friends and loved ones sharing my joy . . .
Smiles, laughter, love, life . . .
I count them one and all!

My blessings . . .
I know . . .
There's a whole lot MORE! ☺

Who I am . . . at 40?

WHO AM I AT 40?

*I am a **NURSE** . . . taking care of patients,*
Running a floor,
Working with people . . .

*I am a **STUDENT** . . . at the University,*
Strivin' hard to learn more, you see . . .

*I am a **FRIEND** . . . you can depend,*
Will cry with you, share a laugh
You can count on me . . . without a doubt! . . .

*I am a **SISTER** . . . who will always stand strong*
And help you carry on,
Give you a helping hand . . .
Be there for you . . . no matter what! . . .

*I am a **WIFE** . . . dedicated and faithful*
To a loving husband . . . who gives me all . . .
Makes me feel loved and cherished,
That I'm not alone . . .
Giving me strength and support I can hold on!

I am a **MOTHER** *. . . of two adorable children . . .*
I'm making feel loved and know about God
Who gives me so much joy
And inspiration to go on . . .
See the world again in the eyes of a child . . .
Rekindle the youth in me . . .
Love and enjoy life!

I am a **DAUGHTER** *. . . fully proud of a father*
Who's been a pillar of strength
All through this time . . .
The echo behind my dreams . . .
The wind beneath my wings!

I am **IMPERFECT,** *but of course*
I get tired, get angered and hurt
a humble **CHILD of God** *. . .*
With values trying to uphold . . .
Trying to keep the faith . . .
Amidst this bewildered, perplexed world!

I am 40 *. . .*
And "life begins", so they say . . .
Another chapter of my life to embrace . . .
The RHYMES in my life
May not always come . . .
But I shall always celebrate . . .
my being . . . A **WOMAN***!*

Why Women Cry

WHY WOMEN CRY

(Unknown)

A little boy asked his mother, "Why are you crying?"
"BECAUSE I'M A WOMAN", she told him.
"I don't understand," he said.
His Mom just hugged him and said,
"And you never will."

Later the little boy asked his father,
"Why does mother seem to cry for no reason?"
"All women cry for no reason," was all his dad could say.

The little boy grew up and became a man,
still wondering why women cry.

Finally, he put in a call to God.
When God got on the phone, he asked,
"God, why do women cry so easily?"

God said, "WHEN I MADE THE WOMAN . . .
SHE HAD TO BE SPECIAL!"

*I made her shoulders STRONG enough
to carry the weight of the world,
Yet GENTLE enough to give comfort.
I gave her an INNER STRENGTH to endure childbirth and
the rejection that many times come from her children.*

*I gave her a HARDNESS that allows her to keep going
when everyone else gives up, and take care of her family
through sickness and fatigue without complaining.*

*I gave her the SENSITIVITY TO LOVE her children
under any and all circumstances,
even when her child has hurt her very badly.*

*I gave her STRENGTH to carry her husband
through his faults and fashioned her
from his rib to protect his heart.*

*I gave her WISDOM to know that a good husband
never hurts his wife,
but sometimes tests her strengths and
her resolve to stand beside him unfalteringly.*

And finally, "I GAVE HER A TEAR TO SHED."

This is hers exclusively to use whenever it is needed."
"You see my son," said God,

"The BEAUTY of a WOMAN is NOT in the
Clothes she wears,
The figure that she carries
Or the way she combs her hair . . .
The BEAUTY of a WOMAN
must be seen in her EYES . . .
Because that is the doorway to her HEART . . .
. . . the place where LOVE resides!"